ULTIMATE FACILITATION TOOL KIT

SECOND EDITION

katherine
rosback

© Copyright 2018, 2020, 2023

2nd EDITION

By Katherine Rosback

All rights reserved.

Printed in the United States.

Cover artwork by Annette Wood

Rosback, Katherine.

Ultimate Facilitation Tool Kit

ISBN 979-8-218-95108-5

For permission to reproduce selections from this book or to obtain information on holding workshops on this topic, visit www.katherinerosback.com.

"Tools always serve the question you are trying to answer."

Katherine Rosback

Scan here to access an audio file that describes the use and organization of this tool kit.

TABLE OF CONTENTS

1	INTRODUCTION
2	TOOL PURPOSES
4	ADI
6	Affinity Diagram
8	ALU
10	Brainwriting
12	Concept Fan
14	Contingency Diagram
16	Data-Finding Matrix
18	Decision Hierarchy
20	Evaluation Grid
22	Fishbone / Batbone
24	Five Whys
26	Flowscape
28	Force Field Analysis
30	Innovation Transfer
32	Is/Is Not
34	IWWM Statements
36	Ladder of Inference
38	Left-Hand Column
40	Multi-Voting
42	Order of Go
44	Random Word
46	SCAMPER
48	Spider Diagram
50	Strategy Table
52	Three-Column Clarifier
54	Values Map

Introduction

Regarding Tools

Working through complex decisions or tough problems with groups of people is an important and challenging task. To assist in this endeavor, this book contains a cadre of tools to aid meetings and workshops designed to address the many analytical problem-solving, decision-making, and innovation initiatives organizations seek to implement.

I have successfully used these tools for more than two decades and in hundreds of "must succeed" meetings in a variety of industries and with all levels of the organizational hierarchy. My goal is that these tools will help you surface new insights, negotiate different perspectives, improve problem-framing, break old patterns of circular meeting talk, engage your participants in deeper thinking, and most importantly, achieve better outcomes.

A few words about tool usage: First, it is vital to remember that tools always serve the question you are trying to answer. Do you know what that question is? If you don't, your tool becomes a "check-the-box" exercise that produces no useful outcomes. Always know what question you are trying to answer, and then pick your tool.

Second, you don't have to name or teach the tool you are about to use. In fact, I advise against it! The reason is you may move the participant's attention out of the flow of the thinking and into the mechanics of the thinking. You then run the risk of people debating the value of the tool, questioning how it really works, and a host of other derailers. So, don't go there. Just use it!

With best wishes for many
successful meeting outcomes,

Katherine Rosback

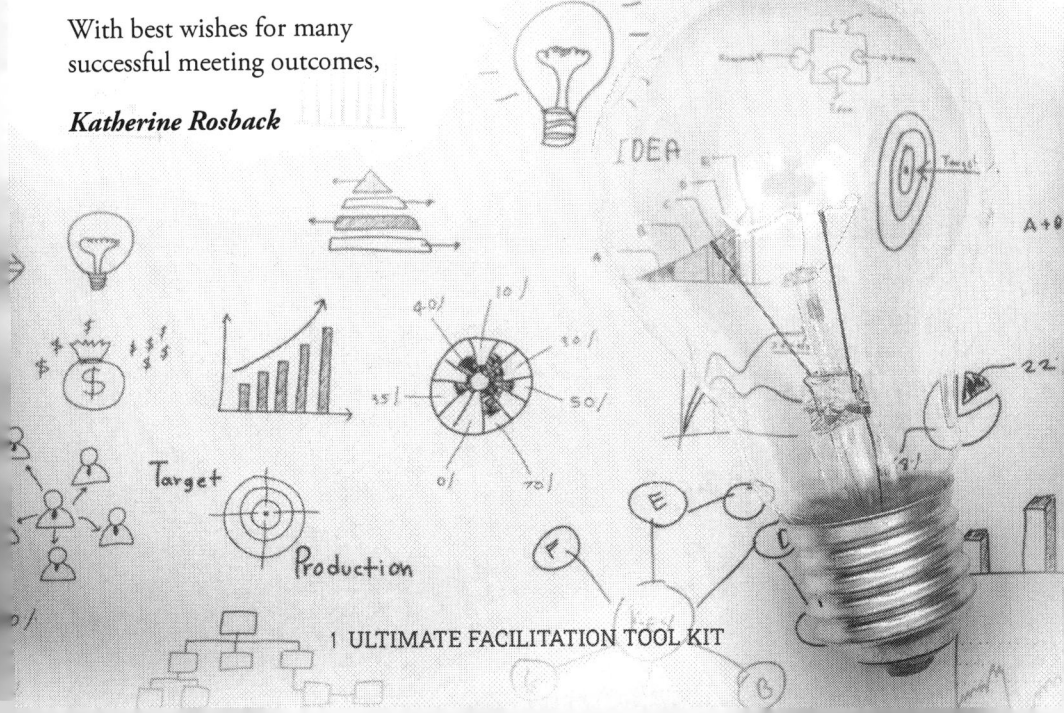

Tool Purposes

Tool	Purpose
ADI	Converge around key areas of thought after a discussion to create truly group-generated consensus
Affinity Diagram	Analyze results of a focus-group discussion, identify problem focus, develop a presentation, or plan a meeting
ALU	Quickly assess 2–4 proposals or options when criteria have not been set in advance
Brainwriting	Diverge on ideas; use this prior to collecting thoughts, use it to start your meeting
Concept Fan	Create new ideas by building on concepts imbedded in initial ideas
Contingency Diagram	Create new ideas by using thoughts on how to make it worse
Data-Finding Matrix	Conduct fact-finding exercises
Decision Hierarchy	Frame a strategic planning initiative, or set discussion boundaries
Evaluation Grid	Assess 3–6 proposals or options with specific criteria, and summarize consequences of making a choice
Fishbone / Batbone	Analyze root causes and root symptoms
Five Whys	Analyze root causes of an issue
Flowscape	Reveal underlying drivers, identify what is critical to a person
Force Field Analysis	Identify the assistors and resistors when implementing a proposal

2 ULTIMATE FACILITATION TOOL KIT

Innovation Transfer 🔊	Create new ideas based on other past successes
Is/Is Not	Frame the focus of a meeting or scope of a project
IWWM Statements	Develop problem statements, or diverge on strategic questions
Ladder of Inference 🔊	Gain insight into the underlying thinking behind a person's statement or action
Left-Hand Column	Understand or reveal hidden agendas, gain insight into how an issue is being framed, analyze a conversation
Multi-Voting	Narrow a long list of options down to the vital few
Order of Go	Improve engagement, increase participation on virtual calls, mitigate impact of naysayers or dominant voices, create inclusion
Random Word 🔊	Create new ideas with metaphors
SCAMPER 🔊	Create new ideas with prompting questions
Spider Diagram	Develop strategic themes
Strategy Table 🔊	Create multiple strategic options
3-Column Clarifier 🔊	Debundle circular talk on what people want, why they want it, and what is stopping them from implementing their ideas
Values Map 🔊	Identify objectives, and visualize the relationship between those objectives

ADI

Tool Purpose

ADI stands for "Agreement, Disagreement, and Irrelevance" and is an invaluable tool in helping teams to "debundle" conflicts and/or to summarize assessments of ideas or alternatives. It does so by breaking down the specifics of the conversation into areas where the group is in agreement, the specific points of their disagreement (or differences of thought), and the points that have no bearing on the topic at hand (irrelevant). Often groups think they can't agree on anything, so this tool assists in illuminating that there are some points of agreement, no matter how small they might be! As it is a converging tool, it must be used after the group has had an in-depth discussion on an issue or topic. This tool can be used at any stage of a problem-solving or decision-making process.

Construction Steps

1. As shown in the illustration, draw the three areas to be explored on a large piece of paper, a whiteboard, or a projection slide.

2. After your team has had some discussion (e.g., with open dialogue, the ALU tool, the Evaluation Grid, or the Affinity Diagram), ask the team, "Where did you hear areas of agreement? We'll list these in the 'Agreement' column." or "What did you hear that was similar between the views presented?"

3. As you discuss what is stated and if everyone agrees with the proffered observations, write that item in the "Agreement" column. Any item that does not receive 100% of the team's agreement must be moved to the "Disagreement" column.

4. Then ask, "Where did we see things differently? Is that disagreement pertinent to the issue we want to resolve?" Capture those items that are pertinent in the "Disagreement" column and those that fall outside the discussion in the "Irrelevant" space.

AGREEMENT	DISAGREEMENT
Need to minimize employee backlash	Use our IT or use a third party?
Must be able to reach a live voice at some point	Use of cloud?
Have to meet corporate cost reduction targets	
(Implementation timeframe) →	

IRRELEVANCE
Where the group should report

Tips for Use

- Use this tool only to summarize the results of a discussion. Do not attempt to use this before (or in place of) a significant dialogue regarding the issue that has taken place.

- If strong differences of opinion exist, begin the exercise by completing the "Agreement" column and possibly leaving some partial agreements in the column. This often surprises factions within the group when they see how much they actually agree on!

- Ask the group to step back and observe their thinking once the exercise has been completed, and then ask, "What have we learned?"

I Am Right, You Are Wrong, by Dr. Edward de Bono

5 ULTIMATE FACILITATION TOOL KIT

Affinity Diagram

Tool Purpose:

The Affinity Diagram is a tool used to identify overarching themes regarding a certain issue or question. It uses inductive thinking as opposed to the more prevalent deductive thinking used in the West. Inductive thinking builds from the bottom up using ideas, questions, thoughts, issues, complaints, and anything else participants can write to organize a multitude of issues into categories the group can address. As such, it is a wonderful tool to use at the start of a messy project when you don't know where to start amidst 100 issues and concerns.

It is also a powerful tool in creating alignment regarding the top themes to address as everyone is *simultaneously* involved in the shaping of the themes. And because these themes are shaped by movement rather than by voice, the dominant voices in the room are not driving the effort!

Construction Steps

1. Attach 2-3 large sticky sheets or have access to a large whiteboard.
2. Ask team members to Brainwrite ideas (see pages 10-11 for how to Brainwrite) independently on individual 3" x 3" sticky notes.
3. Going one-at-a-time, call for team members to read each idea they have written. Ask them to come up to the whiteboard and place their sticky notes in random fashion on the whiteboard.
4. When all ideas have been read and posted, direct team members to simultaneously come to the board and silently sort the sticky notes into groups.
5. After the sorting is complete, work with the team to develop 1-2 labels or themes for each grouping.

Q: HOW TO IMPROVE PRODUCTION CASH FLOW?

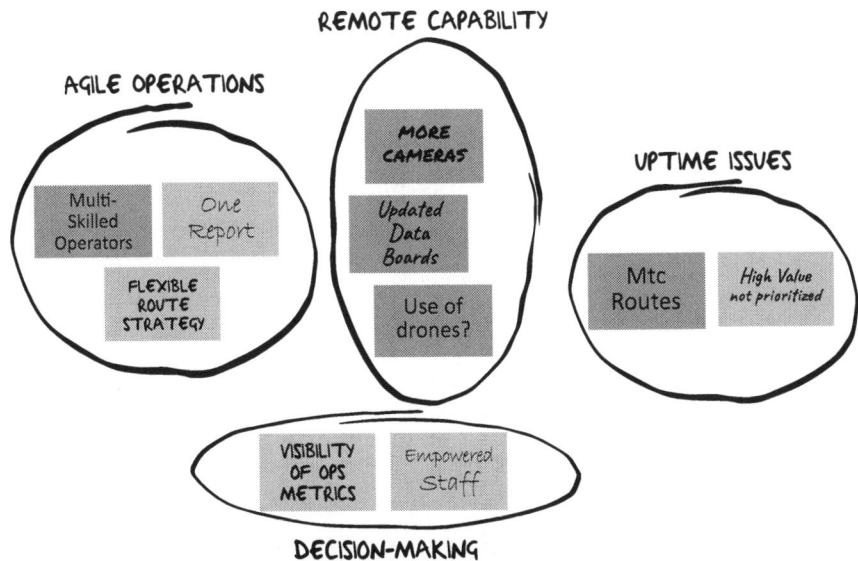

Tips for Use

- Resist the team's temptation to converge — the diagram should result in a minimum of 8–10 groupings.

- Expect an initial flurry of activity followed by an apparent withdrawal when conducting the grouping exercise. Allow this to occur, but then push for re-engagement to move the team to a new plane of thinking.

- Allow teams to duplicate ideas if the ideas fit in more than one grouping (note that this does not happen frequently).

- Communicate that each grouping can have more than one label or theme. Write two themes, and then move on to the next grouping.

- Push for nontraditional groupings; sticky notes should not be grouped according to preexisting ideas.

- Groupings of one sticky note are fine!

Management for Quality Improvement, edited by Shigeru Mizuno

ALU

Tool Purpose

The ALU tool is used to qualitatively assess a set of proposals, options, or strategies. Use it to examine the *Advantages, Limitations,* and *Unique Connections* of a given idea. Its strength over traditional assessment tools is that it sets a specific structure for how something will be assessed. The structure suggested results in balanced thinking instead of the all-too-often discussion that simply focuses on what is wrong with an idea. It also challenges participants to consider additional uses for a particular idea beyond what's currently being discussed. The other key strength of this tool is creating parallel thinking in the group. Parallel thinking is when, at a given moment, the entire group is focusing on the exact same question (e.g., upsides of Option A or downsides of Option B).

Construction Steps

1. Identify the idea, proposal, or set of strategic options that is being considered.
2. Ask the group, "What advantages does this idea offer? What makes it attractive or appealing? What are its strong points?" Record the responses on a large sheet of paper or whiteboard and call it "Advantages."
3. Next, ask the group, "What are the weaknesses or flaws? Are there possible trouble spots? What are the limitations?" Record the responses on a large sheet of paper or a whiteboard and call it "Limitations."
4. Finally, ask the group, "What connections does this option suggest? Are there any hidden potentials?" These should be recorded under the heading "Unique Connections."
5. Identify key areas of difference and/or different understanding (e.g., someone thinks it is an advantage, and someone sees it as a limitation).
6. If you are assessing more than one proposal, complete the positive assessment for all proposals prior to discussing the limitations.

ADVANTAGES	LIMITATIONS
PROPOSED ORGANIZATION REQUIRES FEWER PEOPLE	REQUIRES BROADER SKILL SET
MORE CLOSELY ALIGNED TO CLIENT NEEDS	MORE TRAINING WILL BE NEEDED
UNIQUE CONNECTIONS	
COULD THIS BE USED FOR NEW PROJECT TEAMS?	

Tips for Use

- Indicate an Order of Go when capturing input for both columns (for Order of Go, see pages 42–43). This ensures everyone contributes to each column (rather than waiting to comment on their favorite one).

- Always begin with the Advantages side. Our brains are quite adept at critical thinking, so if the group begins with identifying limitations, they might find it harder to see anything good about an option.

- Ask the group to step back once the exercise is completed to objectively examine the thinking that has taken place.

- Never begin this exercise by listing all comments on a proposal or idea and separating them into the categories. The object of this exercise is a structured group assessment.

- If the group is unable to come up with limitations, ask them to imagine that they have just come back from the future and know that the proposed idea did not work. Ask them to diverge on why it didn't.

Creative Problem Solving, S. Isaken & D. Treffinger

Brainwriting

Tool Purpose

Brainwriting is a diverging tool used to draw out people's ideas, thoughts, concerns, and questions (anything that is on their mind) about a given topic or issue. Brainwriting requires that they first *write* their ideas and then read what they have written. By writing an idea down first, Brainwriting is a powerful tool for (a) mitigating a group's tendency to repeat what others have stated (known as groupthink), (b) lessening the effect of cognitive biases such as the anchoring bias (what I say is "anchored" on what was said or done earlier), and (c) ensuring people don't change their minds because of something a higher-up individual or expert stated prior to their turn to speak. Brainwriting can be used at any stage of problem-solving or decision-making and in conjunction with a variety of tools.

Construction Steps

1. Identify the topic or question (e.g., "What criteria should we consider?" or "What are all the ways we can reduce costs?" or "What are the current perspectives on our problem?").

2. Give each person paper (people tend not to carry paper around these days and writing on paper makes a difference), and ask them to write as many ideas or thoughts on the posed question as possible during a 30-second to 2-minute period.

3. (Optional) Have each group member pass their paper to the person to their left, and then ask them to build on what they see.

4. In a round-robin fashion, ask each person to read what they have written. Record their responses, using their exact words.

5. Continue as a group to add more ideas to the list.

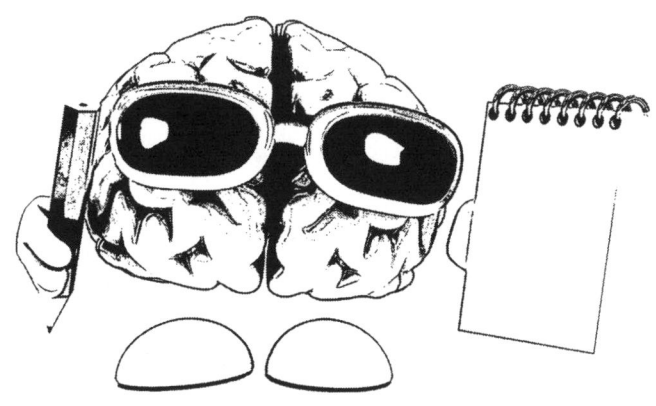

Tips for Use

- One of the most valuable aspects of Brainwriting is that it builds on the principle called cognitive dissonance. People are less likely to change their minds once they have written something down. All too often in meetings people change a thought because of what others say, perhaps because that someone was a boss or the idea was different from other statements. Writing lessens the likelihood that they discard their initial thoughts.

- Define an Order of Go (see definition on page 9) when capturing what team members have written rather than just ask for volunteers to start. For instance, say, "Let's start with you, Pam, and go clockwise around the room."

- If capturing ideas in a round-robin fashion, limit each to reading one thought at a time. This keeps strong personalities from dominating the conversation and ensures more balanced input. "Read off one of the items that you have written, and then we will come back around to see what has been missed."

- This is an excellent tool to break the ice at the start of meetings when you ask a question and everyone just stares back at you (crickets-chirping moment).

- Write down whatever the participant states, even if it has been written before. Consolidate the list later, not during the divergent part of the meeting.

Concept Fan

Tool Purpose

The Concept Fan is a creative thinking tool that helps a group widen the search for solutions by identifying a broader perspective of an initial idea. Thus, it can help move a team beyond the used-too-often favorite solution. The Concept Fan is an excellent tool to use when the initially developed ideas seem impractical or insufficient to address the issue. Rather than toss ideas to the side, the tool guides a team in stepping back to examine the underlying concept that can then be used to create additional ideas.

Construction Steps

1. Write down 5–10 ideas for solving a problem on the left-hand side of a large sheet of paper or whiteboard.
2. Direct the group's attention to one item on the list they have created and ask, "What broad approach is represented by this idea? What does this idea achieve?" Write their responses in a column to the right of their initial ideas.
3. Choose one concept and ask, "What other ideas would make this concept work? How else might we achieve the same purpose?"
4. Write those additional ideas on the left-hand side of the paper or whiteboard.
5. At this point, you can go back and conduct the same exercise from the set of initial 5–10 ideas, or take one of the new ideas generated and ask again, "What does this idea do? What does it acheive? What are other ways to achieve that same outcome?"
6. Keep building on ideas and concepts.

ISSUE: OPERATIONS NOT AWARE OF STATUS ON REQUESTED MAINTENANCE PROJECTS

SPECIFIC IDEA
DISCUSS PROJECT STATUS IN WEEKLY MEETING

BROADER CONCEPT
ENSURE AWARENESS OF PROJECT STATUS

OTHER IDEAS
- EMAIL UPDATES TO AFFECTED PARTIES
- IPHONE NOTIFICATIONS
- PROJECT STATUS LOOK-UP
- INCLUDE WITH OTHER REPORTS
- QUICK QUERY ON PROJECT PAGE?

Tips for Use

- Tape 2–3 large sheets of paper together on the wall or use a large whiteboard for this exercise. You'll need the writing room!
- Don't try to clean up the charts as you move along. Instead, use arrows to precisely display the thinking process that took place and to provide helpful connections during a subsequent idea review.
- Push for broad concepts (e.g., get fit) as they lead to multiple specific ideas (e.g., eat more salads, walk up stairs).
- To work from specifics to broader perspectives, take an idea (e.g., send out pre-reads) and ask, "What broader concept could be governing this idea? What does this idea achieve?" This can lead to responses such as "Shortens meeting time" or "Improves meeting focus." You then ask, "How else might we shorten the meeting time?" This should lead to a whole set of other ideas!

Serious Creativity, Edward de Bono

Contingency Diagram

Tool Purpose

The Contingency Diagram is a creative thinking tool that creates design alternatives, identifies solutions to a given problem, or pinpoints strategic alternatives. This idea generation tool plays upon a key brain strength – to critique. Our brains exhibit a powerful ability to identify what can go wrong. The Contingency Diagram tool leverages that ability by first identifying how to make our area of focus worse. That list is then used as a springboard to identify ways in which the situation or task can be improved.

Construction Steps

1. Draw the picture shown on the next page on a large sheet of paper or whiteboard.
2. Select the problem or issue you would like to address.
3. Write the opposite of the selected topic in the circle. If you are looking to make a process more effective, the question might be, "How can we make this process more ineffective?" If you are wanting to develop a new product, the question might be, "How can we ensure that no one would ever want to buy this product?"
4. Brainstorm all the possible ways to make the negative reframing happen. (Groups tend to love this part!)
5. Once a good list is generated, circle one of the negative ideas and ask, "What would be the opposite of this negative idea? What does that suggest? What is this idea trying to achieve? How else might we achieve this? Enable this?"
6. Continue this process until the list of negatives has been reversed into a list of positive actions.

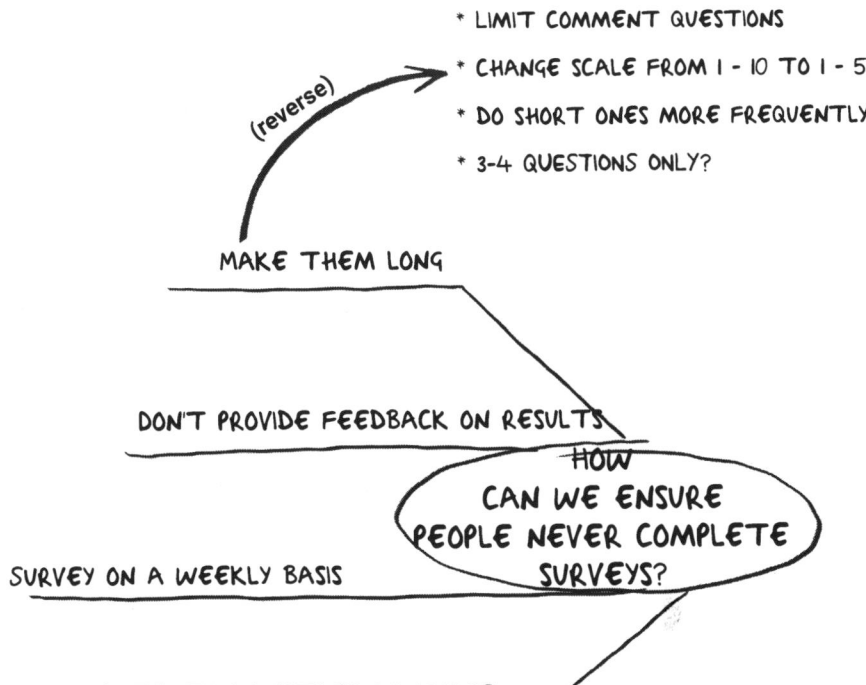

Tips for Use

- Specificity is important. Therefore, ensure that your negative problem statement is succinct. Push the group for specific negatives with questions such as "What are we trying to do here?"
- Look for concepts among the negative statements before reversing them into positives. Ask, "What's the broader perspective behind this?"
- List all possible ways to perpetuate an undesirable state, and then phrase the reverse of the negative by asking, "In what ways might..."
- Avoid a one-to-one transfer of negative ideas to positives as often as you can. Generate multiple positives ideas for one "how to make it worse" idea.

Data-Finding Matrix

Tool Purpose

A team, like a good detective, should initially be open to discussing all possible data and information sources when framing their problem statement or strategic question. All too often, however, a team dives prematurely into one aspect and loses the opportunity to develop a more comprehensive view of what it is they want to resolve. The Data-Finding Matrix is a diverging tool that assists a team in exploring all possible data sources. In addition, it focuses subsequent data collection efforts by sorting data into known (readily available information) or need to know (data that needs testing, questioning, or research).

This tool is most often used early in a problem-solving or decision-making process as it grounds the group on the set of knowns and unknowns. It should definitely be used prior to the development of the problem statement or strategic question.

Construction Steps

1. Diverge on the questions that need to be answered in order to address your issue, be it to better understand a decision you are facing or to frame the problem you want to solve. Use the who-what-where-when-why-how labeling as prompts.

2. Focus on one question at a time, and ask, "Is this something we know or that we need to know?" Discuss the responses, and based on the results of the discussion, move the question into either the "Know" or "Need to Know" column.

3. Begin first with the "Know" questions, and capture the responses to those questions from the group. If there are conflicting responses or debate as to what the answer is, move the question to the "Need to Know" column.

4. Next, move to the "Need to Know" questions, and identify how you will obtain the information that will answer those question. Note that this should include who will be the source of that information.

	KNOW	NEED TO KNOW
WHO	WHO IS OR ISN'T INVOLVED? WHO MIGHT HAVE INFORMATION THAT WE DON'T HAVE? WHO ARE THE OTHER INVOLVED GROUPS?	
WHAT	WHAT ARE THE SYMPTOMS OF THIS MESS? WHAT'S THE GOAL? WHAT ASPECTS ARE CONSIDERED A CRISIS? WHAT DISADVANTAGES EXIST FOR SOLVING THIS MESS? WHAT SUCCESSES HAVE WE ACHIEVED SO FAR? WHAT DO STAKEHOLDERS THINK ABOUT THIS ISSUE?	
WHERE	WHERE DOES THIS MESS FIRST BECOME OBVIOUS? WHERE IS IT LEAST NOTICEABLE? WHERE HAS THIS HAPPENED BEFORE?	
WHEN	WHEN DO THE SYMPTOMS OCCUR? WHEN DON'T THEY OCCUR?	
WHY	WHY DOES THIS MAKE PERFECT SENSE? WHY ARE OTHER PEOPLE INVOLVED? WHY DOESN'T THIS MESS GO AWAY? WHY DO WE CARE?	
HOW	HOW ARE OTHER GROUPS OR INDIVIDUALS INVOLVED? HOW HAVE OTHERS ADDRESSED THIS?	

Tips for Use

- Organizations abound with precise solutions for the wrong problem. Teams tend to be quick to set their problem frame without fully diverging on what they don't know and being far too confident that what they know is fact. As noted by Mark Twain, "It ain't what you don't know that gets you into trouble. It's what you know for sure that just ain't so."

- Avoid a team's proclivity for wanting to immediately answer a given question. That can result in a long debate on a question that perhaps has little value.

- The Multi-Voting tool (pages 40–41) is a good method to shorten an overwhelming list of questions.

- Use Brainwriting (pages 10–11) to capture everyone's suggested questions in order to minimize the impact of group think and maximize diversity of thought.

Creative Problem-Solving Course, Isaken & Treffinger

Decision Hierarchy

Tool Purpose

The Decision Hierarchy is used to remove ambiguity regarding a team's list of questions that they must answer and ensures alignment on those decisions that are the focus for consideration. Some decisions are givens as they have already been made (for instance, those made by a senior management team). Others are dependent on the choices made for the focus decisions; thus, they can be made later. The Decision Hierarchy clarifies this context. As such, it is an excellent tool to use at the beginning of a project or multi-day working meeting to ensure everyone is in agreement and aligned on the focus for discussion. It is also an excellent deliverable to bring back to a chartering group (such as a decision board) to ensure that the working team has correctly framed the project.

This tool is almost always used at the beginning of a project, problem-solving, or decision-making effort.

Construction Steps

1. On a large sheet of paper or whiteboard, draw a triangle and divide it horizontally into three sections.
2. Label the three sections (from top to bottom): "Decisions Already Made," "Team Focus," and "Decisions to Be Made Later."
3. Ask the team members to Brainwrite (see pages 10–11) their ideas of what belongs in each section.
4. Working one section at a time (it doesn't matter where you start), capture everyone's responses, and note them in that section. Then move on to the next section.
5. When items appear in multiple sections, simply circle them since you will return to address them in the next step.
6. When all sections have been completed through dialogue, discuss and resolve the differences.

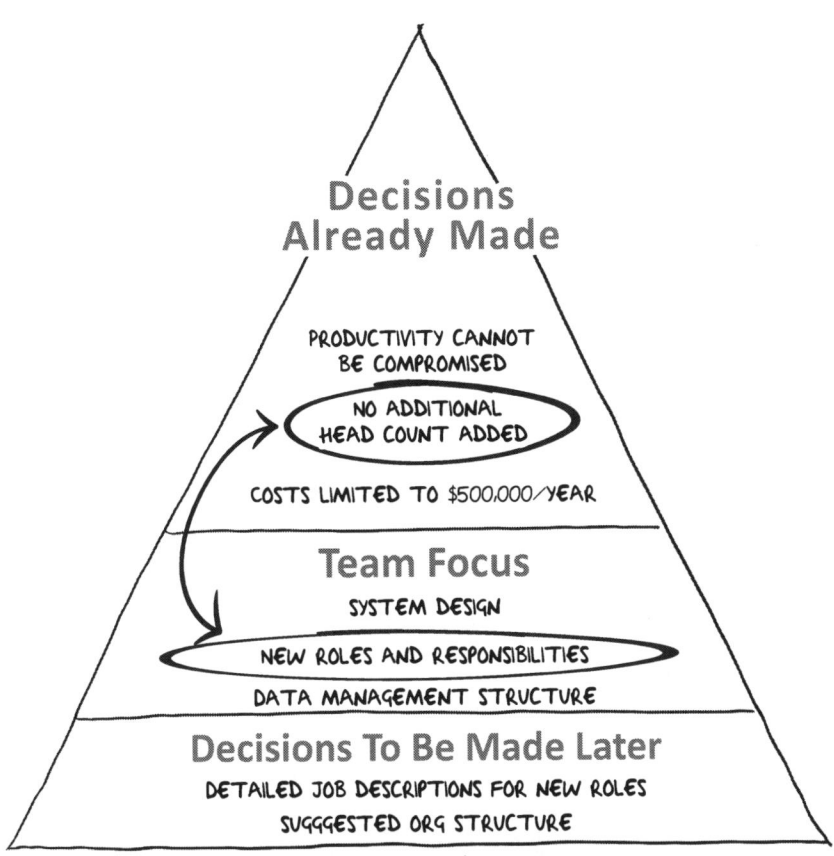

Tips for Use

- If you are already aware of decisions made by upper management on projects, write those in the appropriate section prior to asking the group.
- The purpose of this tool is to initially draw out how people see things differently, so don't be alarmed if one area of focus shows up in two places.
- Avoid the terms "strategic" or "tactical" in labeling the triangle as those terms can carry confusing or negative connotations (people can end up in endless debates on what constitutes "strategic" and what is "tactical").

Decision & Risk Analysis, Kenneth Oppenheimer

Evaluation Grid

Tool Purpose

The Evaluation Grid provides a framework that assists in comparing a set of alternatives when multiple objectives are present. It is a more sophisticated assessment tool than the ALU (see pages 8–9) since teams identify and agree upon evaluation criteria *prior* to any assessment. (The ALU simply asks for advantages and disadvantages with no group consensus on what the most important criteria are.) While some proposed uses of this tool suggest using "add-to-the-winner" and/or weighting factors, I advocate using this tool as a discussion aid that facilitates a balanced comparison of options—one criterion at a time—highlighting areas where they agree and disagree. Note that this tool is insufficient when uncertainty is present (i.e., you won't know the outcome of some given criterion until a time in the future after you have made your choice).

Use this tool after a team has identified a set of possible alternatives. Given that it becomes mentally overwhelming to evaluate more than seven options, it is wise prior to using the ALU tool to narrow down a long list of options.

Construction Steps

1. Brainstorm a list of possible criteria (a) by asking the group, "By what criteria shall we assess these options?" or (b) by directing team members to pick their favorite option and then, without sharing WHAT they chose, describe WHY they chose the option they did (my personal favorite).
2. Discuss each criterion to ensure an aligned, clear, and precise interpretation of what is meant by that criterion.
3. Using Multi-Voting, narrow the list down to 5–7 top choices (for Multi-Voting see pages 40–41).
4. Choose a non-numerical method such as graphics to indicate ranking for subjective criteria, using hard data only when reliable (e.g., distance to the workplace or number of bedrooms in a house).
5. Move vertically through the table, working one criterion at a time.
6. When the table is complete, ask, "Can any alternatives be dropped?" Then ask, "Where did we *disagree* on our assessments?" Circle those items, and then one by one explore the underlying thinking using a tool such as the Ladder of Inference to either arrive at an aligned assessment or identify an outcome that needs further investigation.

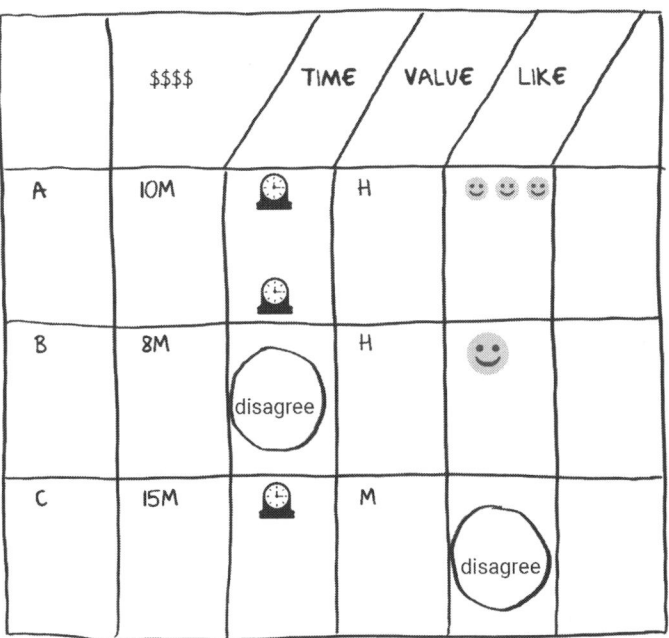

Tips for Use

- Work the grid one criterion at a time so you can compare all ideas to a single criterion. This is especially important when working with subjective criteria or those criteria for which we have no "hard" data.
- Do not sum to determine the winner. Rather, use the results to examine strengths and weaknesses of the options. Circle boxes that create simultaneous responses such as "I say high!" and "I say low!" Work them later, after you have completed the entire grid.
- Numerical ranking is not the objective of this exercise! The objective is to hold a structured, balanced assessment of each option.
- Use check marks, emojis, dollar signs, and so on as opposed to numbers (except where hard numbers such as a distance to a place are available and known).
- If you are working with subjective criteria such as value, do not average assessments of value. If someone states it is of high value and someone states it is of low value, it would be inaccurate to average those responses.

Adapted from the Criteria Grid by K. Rosback. See also *Smart Choices* and the Consequences Table by J. Hammond, R. Keeney, and H. Raiffa and "Problems with Scoring Methods and Ordinal Scales in Risk Assessment" by D. Hubbard and D. Evans (2010) in *IBM J. RES. & DEV.* VOL. 54 NO. 3.

Fishbone / Batbone

Tool Purpose

The Fishbone diagram, also known as the cause-and-effect diagram, helps a group diverge on all potential causes of a problem or issue. This is a deductive tool in that we work from predetermined high-level themes to underlying specifics. The pre-labeled bones of the fish connected to the main bone become categories that facilitate a team's ability to fully diverge on all possible causes rather than prematurely focusing on familiar or surface causes. It is a powerful visual that illustrates connections and sub-causes and is very easy to use.

Construction Steps

1. Write the problem in a box on the far right side of a large sheet of paper or whiteboard.
2. Draw a horizontal line to this box, and draw 4–5 fishbones off of this primary line.
3. Label these with high-level cause categories. These can be the 5 M's (man, machine, method, material, measurement) or the 4 P's (policies, procedures, people, plant). The team can also choose to create their own high-level categories.
4. Focusing on one high-level category at a time, begin brainstorming possible causes. Record the idea on the appropriate rib.
5. Continue to break down the possible causes by using the Five Whys technique (see pages 24–25).
6. Using Multi-Voting, identify the most likely causes.

The Batbone

One of the more predictable happenings when using the fishbone diagram is that groups capture *symptoms* instead of *causes* of a given issue. A cause is a contributing reason, a sub-problem, or a limiting factor for why the issue or "mess" exists, whereas a symptom is an observable phenomenon arising from the *existence* of that issue. For instance, if you have a cold, a runny nose is a symptom of having contracted the cold virus while a cause can be along the lines of "failure to wear a mask around a colleague who has a cold" or "compromised immune system." Another example of symptoms versus causes might be observable behaviors such as operators taking safety risks or an operations person feeling overwhelmed after a new process has been implemented. In this example, a poor process design or lack of training in the new process might be the causes, and the two behaviors noted above are symptoms of those failures.

Confusing symptoms with causes is a major reason for what is known as a Type III error, solving the wrong problem precisely. The Batbone helps mitigate that common flaw when framing problems.

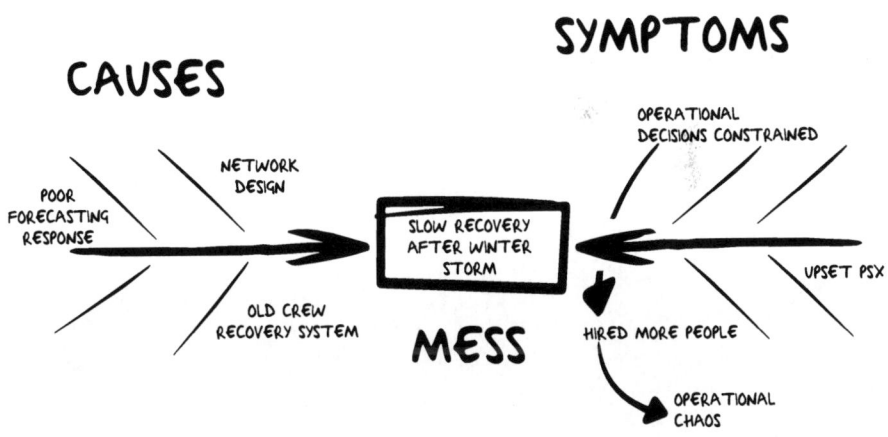

Dr. Kaoru Ishikawa, 1943/K. Rosback, 1994

23 ULTIMATE FACILITATION TOOL KIT

Five Whys

(Video Link)

Tool Purpose

The Five Whys is a simple problem-solving technique to help individuals or groups identify a root cause. By continuing to ask the why question, this tool moves a group past the tendency to focus on symptoms or the initial presenting issue rather than root causes. While the tool is easy to learn and apply, it is not a strong diverging tool as it can lead a group down one pathway of thinking, focusing on one particular cause rather than exploring a range of possible contributing factors (such as with the Fishbone Diagram).

Construction Steps

1. Write the problem or issue in the middle of a large sheet of paper or whiteboard.
2. Ask, "Why does this mess or issue exist?"
3. Capture all the responses as offshoots of the original issue.
4. Circle one response and ask, "Why does this cause exist?" Write down the responses (there will likely be more than one).
5. Circle one of these responses and ask, "If this cause was corrected, is it likely the problem would recur?" If the answer is yes, it is likely this is a contributing factor, not a root cause. Thus, continue peeling back the onion by asking questions such as, "Why does this happen?" or "Why does it make perfect sense that this exists?"
6. Repeat Steps 4–5 until the group has fully diverged on the issue and they feel they have arrived at a root cause that, if solved, would keep the problem from reoccuring.
7. (Optional) Select the top possible causes using the Multi-Voting tool (see pages 40–41).

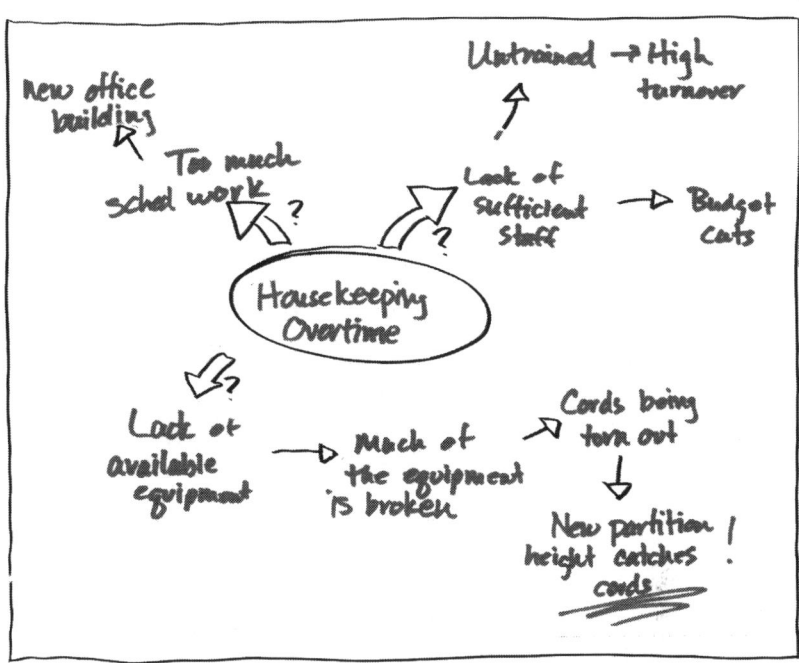

Tips for Use

- Place 2–3 large sheets of paper on the wall, or use a whiteboard. Write the problem or issue in the center. Capture all group responses to the "Why is this the case?" or "Why is this happening?" questions by circling out from that center.

- If the process fails to quickly identify a root cause, you might be dealing with a much more complex problem than this tool can assist in answering. Don't hesitate to put this tool aside for a more sophisticated analytical tool such as a statistical analysis.

- Sometimes it can take less than asking why five times. Sometimes it can take more. So don't let the tool name confine your thinking!

Toyota Production Systems, 1970s

Flowscape

Tool Purpose

Using this tool is not for the faint of heart. Flowscape is an incredibly powerful tool for visualizing the "flow of the thinking" of a person's inner world of values or objectives. Through the illustration of loops and connections, it uncovers the fundamental perceptions that dominate a person's thinking. It is used to understand how a person has organized his or her mental views regarding a particular topic or issue and the values that will be driving their thinking. This tool is not intended to uncover "truth" or what is right or wrong. Rather, it is used to uncover what is, to understand why people see a particular situation so differently, and to understand what values shape their reasoning processes.

This tool is most often used near the beginning of a workshop. The outputs of this exercise can be used as inputs to a Values Map (see pages 54–55).

Construction Steps

1. Identify the subject for the Flowscape.
2. Have each group member write 8–15 letters in alphabetical order down the left-hand side of a piece of paper.
3. Ask each person to write their top-of-mind thoughts—characteristics, impressions, and ideas—about the situation next to each letter, using no more than five words.
4. Direct persons to identify an item on their list and ask, "To which other item on your list does this lead to? Have an affinity for?" Write the letter that corresponds to that item on the right-hand side of the chosen item. (You will now have a letter on both sides of the item you just considered.)
5. Continue this process for all other items on the list.
6. Draw a map showing the directional flow of all items and the relationship between all of the thoughts and/or values initially listed.
7. Examining your resulting map, highlight the letters that "collect" multiple arrows from other points. Highlight the items that are involved in loops.
8. With the group, share and explore which items were involved in loops or had multiple arrows pointing to it. Ask, "Where were we different? Similar?" or "As we compare our indivdual results, what does this suggest about how the group should proceed? Reveal about our values?"

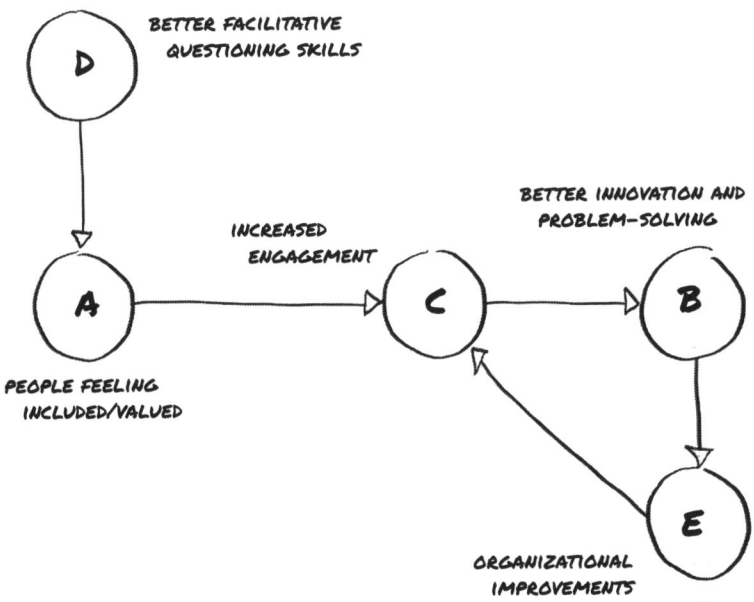

Tips for Use

- To effectively facilitate this tool, it is strongly advised to first practice it to examine your own flow of thinking.
- Multiple items on the list can flow to the same item (e.g., both A and D can flow to F). One item can only flow to one other item (e.g., A can only flow to C, not to C and F).
- It is possible to have more than one loop. There can be 2–3 totally separate loops!
- This is not a cause-and-effect diagram, so avoid the temptation to demand a proven relationship in indicating the flow. This is only a picture of our perceptions at this moment.
- Sometimes lead-to items are not immediately obvious. This may indicate a longer list is needed, but in any case, ask the individual to do their best. Urge them to find a connection that "best fits."

Water Logic, Edward de Bono

Force Field Analysis

Tool Purpose

The Force Field tool (also known as the Assistors/Resistors tool) is an excellent change management tool that visually depicts the people, timing, organizational components, and other forces that hinder or help with the implementation of up-take of an initiative or decision. The output of the tool can be used as inputs for an implementation plan or contingency plan (how we will react if something goes wrong). The key value of this tool is that it assists a group in identifying underlying cultural and behavioral forces that can interfere with implementation of organizational initiatives or strategic plans. These variables must be considered.

Construction Steps

1. Draw a large T on a large sheet of paper or a whiteboard.
2. Write "Current State" at the top left of the T along with a brief description.
3. Write "Desired State" at the top right of the T along with a brief description.
4. In the left column, list the people, events, and timing that will assist the proposed change.
5. After completing the left column, record in the right column the people, events, and timing that will resist the proposed change.
6. Examining the assistors list, develop plans on how to leverage those forces or perhaps how to add even more assistors.
7. With regard to resistors, discuss ways these forces can be minimized, mitigated, leveraged, or eliminated. It is also revealing to ask, "Why does it make perfect sense that Resistor XXX even exists? What does this achieve?"

ASSISTORS	RESISTORS
WHAT SYMPTOM GOES AWAY WHEN THIS IS FIXED?	WHO MIGHT OPPOSE THIS?
WHAT CULTURAL COMPONENTS WILL HELP ENABLE THIS?	WHAT CULTURAL ASPECTS?
WHO WILL BENEFIT FROM THIS?	WHAT POWER STRUCTURES WILL BE CHALLENGED?
WHO IN THE ORGANIZATION SUPPORTS THIS?	WHAT DEPARTMENTS WILL RESIST?
WHY SHOULD WE DO THIS?	WHAT CHANGES WILL PEOPLE HAVE TO MAKE? GIVE UP?
WHAT PROBLEM DOES THIS SOLVE? WHO CARES THAT IT IS SOLVED?	WHAT TIME OF YEAR WILL NOT BE A GOOD ONE TO IMPLEMENT?

Tips for Use

- It is often helpful to begin with the driving forces or assistors.
- Discourage groups from switching back and forth between columns.
- If something is a powerful force, write it in larger letters to demonstrate the weight it carries.
- After completing both columns, ask the group to evaluate the final results with questions such as, "What's your gut feeling about the resulting balances?" "Do you feel that it's worthwhile to proceed?" "What does this tell us about going ahead with the implementation of this proposal?"
- If the conclusion from the group is to move ahead with the plan, assess how the restraining forces can be overcome. Ask, "What are some ways this resistor can be mitigated? Who might be someone we can pull in to help us address this?"

The Creative Edge, William C. Miller

Innovation Transfer

Tool Purpose

This creative thinking tool builds upon the mind's wonderful ability to make connections from past experiences. Rather than simply brainstorming new ideas to solve an issue, the Innovation Transfer tool leverages lessons learned from past situations. The concepts from the list of past situations are then used to generate a list of possible solutions that might address the current situation.

Construction Steps

1. Divide a large sheet of paper or whiteboard into two columns.
2. At the top of the righ-hand side, write "Current Situation," and describe the current issue or problem.
3. Ask the group for feelings and reactions to the current situation, and write those on a second large sheet of paper or whiteboard.
4. In 2–3 minutes, have the group brainstorm a list of past situations that elicited the same feelings (but don't necessarily have a connection to the current problem).
5. Circle one of the situations that most members of the group identify with, and write that situation on the left-hand side of the two-columned large sheet of paper or whiteboard.
6. Ask the group, "How did you solve or deal with the past situation?" and list those responses in the left-hand column.
7. Transfer these solution concepts to the current situation by asking, "How might we use these same principles to solve our current problem?" or "What does this idea suggest?"

PAST SITUATION	CURRENT SITUATION
THIS REMINDS ME OF OUR LAST COMPANY FISHING TRIP WHEN WE COULD FIND NO FISH!	FALLING SALES
LISTEN FOR OTHER FISHING BOATS, FOLLOW THEM → CHANGE THE BAIT → STAY BY THE CAMPFIRE AND CONSUME BEVERAGES (LOL) → DROP FIRECRACKERS IN THE WATER → STEAL FISH OFF OF OTHER BOATS (OKAY, THIS IS JUST A JOKE BUT WE DID CONSIDER IT)	IMPROVE COMPETITIVE MONITORING SELL IMMEDIATELY AFTER COMPETITION, PREEMPTIVE SELLING? GET THERE FIRST?? CHANGE SALES TACTICS— HOW CAN WE "GRAB" NEW CLIENTS? SALES LITERATURE TO "FLUSH OUT NEW CLIENTS" HIGHLIGHT CURRENT ISSUES?

Tips for Use

- Take no longer than 3 minutes to develop the list of past solutions. Pick the one that resonates best with the group (e.g., you might hear someone remark, "You know, this reminds me of the time when...." Run with that comment!)

- Leave plenty of room between ideas for resolving the past situations while recording them on the large sheet of paper or whiteboard as you will get (or will push for) multiple ideas for each past solution.

- Complete the list of how a past situation was dealt with before you begin to transfer. The tool works best if you do not switch back and forth between columns.

- Resist the group's temptation to transfer the exact idea from one column to the next. The strength of this tool is its ability to produce broader concepts that can be used to generate new ideas.

ULTIMATE FACILITATION TOOL KIT

Is/Is Not

Tool Purpose

The Is/Is Not tool assists groups in defining the boundaries for what should and should not be part of a meeting discussion (very much like the Decision Hierarchy on pages 18–19.) If this is completed at the beginning of a discussion, it refocuses a team back on topic. It also can be used in creating a project charter or framing a problem statement. Teams have also used it to define the list of responsibilities for a particular role. The possibilities are endless! The primary value of this tool is having the team discuss what is not part of the discussion, something that is often not considered. This tool would most frequently be used at the beginning of a problem-solving or decision-making effort.

Construction Steps

1. Divide a large sheet of paper or whiteboard into two columns. Label the top of the left-hand column "IS" and the right-hand column "IS NOT."
2. Ask the team to BRAINWRITE those items that should and should not be part of the discussion.
3. Indicating an Order of Go, collect all responses they generated for the "IS" column. Ask, "What should be part of a given discussion? Project? Decision?"
4. After you have captured all responses on the "IS" side, then collect responses to what should not be part of the discussion.
5. Sometimes a comment will show up in both columns. Simply circle those items that show up on both sides and, upon completion of gathering all responses, seek understanding of why someone saw the comment as something that should be part of the discussion or should not be part of the discussion. Continue that exploration until the comments find a home in either column.

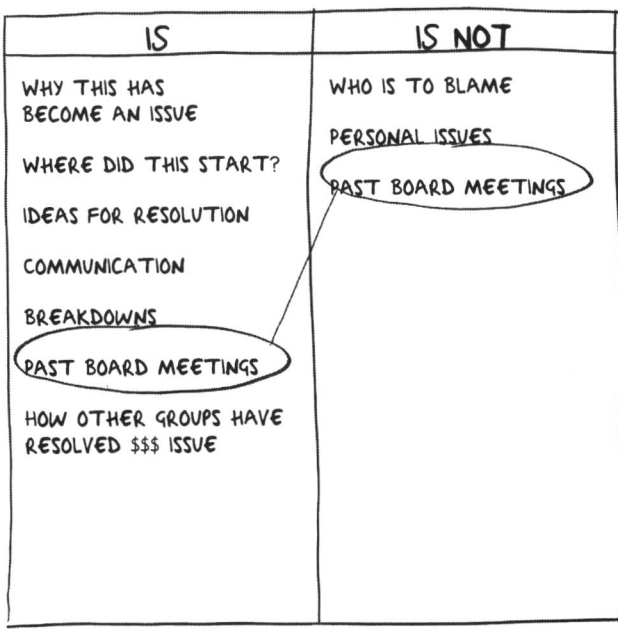

Tips for Use

- Ask each person to write their responses prior to sharing them with the group. This provides valuable insight into how differently the group was thinking about the scope of the presenting issue.

- Do not initially allow people to debate disagreements with what someone else has stated. Simply note that you hear they see it differently and encourage the person to bring up the conflicting point of view when you move to complete the "Is Not" column.

- Expect to see items listed on both sides of the large sheet of paper or whiteboard. Circle those items that appear on both sides, and resolve differences at the end of the exercise. Then use the resulting "Is" statements to define the group charter or problem statement.

The Rational Manager, Charles Kepner and Benjamin Tregoe

IWWM Statements

Tool Purpose

Albert Einstein noted that creativity is rooted in the ability to frame the problem differently, in learning how to ask new questions, to take old problems and examine them in a different way. In this sense, the In What Way Might (IWWM) statement assists teams in diverging on alternative problem definitions. Problem definition is not a simple, mechanical activity; it requires imagination and discovering new perceptions. It is likely one of the most overlooked and underexplored steps in a given problem-solving or decision-making process. Too often teams take a given problem for granted and end up creating a Type III error—solving the wrong problem, precisely.

This tool also makes a statement more solvable by forcing the typical problem statement into the form of a question, a much more powerful way to stimulate ideas for innovative solutions.

Construction Steps

1. Write a general description of the mess/problem on a sheet of paper.
2. Divide a large sheet of paper or whiteboard into two columns. Label the first column "Owner" and the second column "Actions."
3. Ask team members to brainstorm on possible owners of the current issue or identified problem, and write these down.
4. Using the list of actions on the following page, choose five actions that look intriguing, and choose another five actions randomly.
5. Label a second large sheet of paper or whiteboard "Possible Problem Statements," and begin pairing owners with different actions.
6. Multi-Vote to choose the "top" problem statements.

Action Checklist

ORGANIZE	MODIFY	BEGIN
ARRANGE	EXCHANGE	START
ASSEMBLE	ALTER	ESTABLISH
PREPARE	SWITCH	COMMENCE
ORDER	SUBSTITUTE	INITIATE
DISTRIBUTE	ATTEMPT	LAUNCH
SYSTEMATIZE	STRIVE	SATISFY
SCHEDULE	INVENT	APPEASE
SETTLE	CONVEY	EXTEND
GROUP	BECOME	SUPPLY
DEVELOP	ENJOY	AMPLIFY
GENERATE	ENRICH	BUILD
PRODUCE	MOTIVATE	ENLARGE
EVOLVE	ENCOURAGE	REDUCE
DISCLOSE	PROVOKE	INCREASE
EXPRESS	INSPIRE	DECREASE
GROW	RENEW	MAGNIFY
MATURE	REVIVE	PERFORM
ADMIRE	REFRESH	MANAGE
APPROACH	REWARD	ELIMINATE
CONVERGE	IMPROVE	HANDLE
PLAN	AMEND	CONTROL
CHANGE	UPGRADE	

Creative Problem-Solving Course, Isaken & Treffinger

Ladder of Inference

Tool Purpose

The Ladder of Inference tool provides a visual structure for uncovering the underlying thinking for why someone took a particular action or made a certain statement. It is based on the premise that our presenting actions have their roots in our internal perceptual processes that (a) filter what really happened and (b) make corresponding meanings and generalizations about those data. How we make meaning about what we saw or heard is usually based on past experiences, prior knowledge, or cultural filters. Understanding those three filters can explain why a certain statement or action makes perfect sense—at least to that person!

Construction Steps

1. Identify a comment or generalization stated in a meeting.
2. Ask one of the following questions: "What are several possibilities that may have led you to that assumption/conclusion?" or "Can you share more of your thinking on that?"
3. To move down to the next level, you may probe further with questions such as, "What did you observe that led you to that assumption?" or "Can you share a specific instance where you have seen _____?" or "How did you interpret that action when you saw it happen?"

NOTE: This tool is mainly used as a mental model to visually indicate the level at which a person is speaking. You do not have to draw a ladder to use this tool!

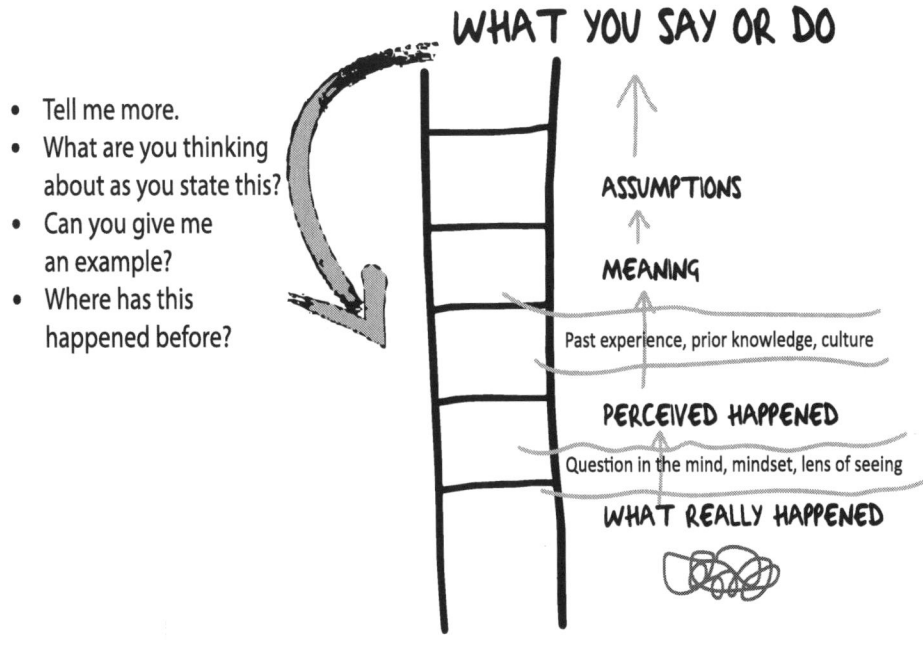

- Tell me more.
- What are you thinking about as you state this?
- Can you give me an example?
- Where has this happened before?

Tips for Use

- Keep the questioning process open-ended. This is not to be used to accuse or diagnose someone.

- Use "how" instead of "why" when beginning the questioning process. It tends to be less inflammatory. For instance ask, "How did you come to that conclusion, Paul?"

- We climb up the Ladder of Inference in milliseconds. Going back down the ladder takes time and thought.

- The fundamental question that the Ladder of Inference answers is, "Why does it make perfect sense that they see the world the way they do?" Your job is to ask the questions that make your conversational partner's thinking visible so your perfect-sense question is answered. Think like a detective!

Overcoming Organizational Defenses, Chris Arygis. See also *The Fifth Discipline Fieldbook*, Peter Senge (ed.)

37 ULTIMATE FACILITATION TOOL KIT

Left-Hand Column

Tool Purpose

The Left-Hand Column (LHC) assists with developing either personal or group awareness of internal assumptions that shape, order, inhibit, and/or frame our conversations. It can be used either by an individual who wants to examine their underlying thinking or feelings that led to responding in a particular way or a facilitator to identify the "undiscussables" present in a group. It is a high-level intervention tool and thus should be used with extreme caution and only with groups who exhibit a high degree of trust in one another.

Construction Steps

1. Select a specific discussion that has been difficult for the group.
2. Instruct each participant to divide a sheet of paper in half.
3. Ask them to rewrite the dialogue to the best of their recall down the right side of their paper in a "he said/she said" format.
4. Ask participants to then write in the left-hand column what they were thinking or feeling *but not saying* for each statement made.
5. Have them reflect on what happened by asking one of the following questions (NOTE: these depend on your goal for the situation):
   - "What led you to think or feel that way?"
   - "What were you really trying to accomplish?"
   - "What prevented you from acting differently?"
   - "What's an assumption you are making that might be challenged?"
   - "What is a different question you might have asked?"

WHAT I WAS THINKING / FEELING	WHAT I SAID
EVERYONE SAID THE STRATEGIC PRESENTATION WAS AWFUL	ME: HOW DID THE REVIEW GO?
DOES HE REALLY NOT KNOW HOW BAD IT WAS? OR IS IT JUST BECAUSE HIS EGO IS ON THE LINE?	JOE: WELL, I'M NOT REALLY SURE - IT WAS HARD TO TELL.
	ME: AS LEADER, WHAT DO YOU THINK WE SHOULD DO? THIS STUFF IS PRETTY IMPORTANT.
	JOE: I CAN'T REALLY SAY - MAYBE WE SHOULD WAIT FOR CONCRETE FEEDBACK.
I CAN'T BELIEVE HE CAN'T SEE HOW THIS HURTS OUR PROJECT. IT'S TIME TO REMOVE HIM AS LEADER	ME: YOU MAY BE RIGHT, BUT I THINK WE NEED TO BE MORE AGGRESSIVE THAN THAT

Tips for Use

- This is a powerful introspection tool that allows courageous individuals to examine their own thinking patterns. It is not necessary, or wise, to share results with the group.
- Sharing results can lead to profound breakthroughs but should not be used with groups who do not show trust.
- To begin the process of addressing the conflict, ask individuals to rewrite the conversation as they might have perceived it. OPTIONAL: Then have them share it with another person (perhaps one who saw the initial conversation) to check for further underlying assumptions.

The Fifth Discipline Fieldbook, Peter Senge, et al. (ed.). Developed by Chris Argyris and Donald Schon.

Multi-Voting

Tool Purpose

Multi-Voting is a prioritization method that narrows a long list of options or ideas down to a manageable few. It is not a pick-the-winner tool. Rather, it identifies the vital few items that a team will further consider. Multi-Voting can be used throughout a given problem-solving or decision-making process, from selecting data sources or converging a list of possible problem statements to selecting the criteria that will be used for assessing solutions.

Its value lies in giving multiple votes to individuals. Unlike being able to place only one vote, having multiple votes allows a person to indicate items that are of great importance to them, and those that would be "nice to have." In essence, multiple votes on a single item captures the weighting factor, something a single vote cannot do.

Construction Steps

1. Combine like ideas. Then discuss each of the ideas so the group has a common level of understanding. (This does not mean that all individuals agree on an item. It simply means all thoughts have been expressed and noted.)
2. Assign each group member 3-5 votes (this depends on the size of the group and the number of items on a list).
3. Have each group member privately cast their assigned number of votes next to the desired items on the list. They may put all votes on the one item on the list that they feel strongly about, or they can spread the votes around.
4. Either have the group members read off their voting preferences, or have them approach the whiteboard and mark their own votes.
5. Tally the total number of votes for each item, and record it next to the item.

POSSIBLE CRITERIA	
༨༨༨	SUPPORTS EDUCATION SUPPORTS ORG. MISSION STATEMENT
I	STRONG ROI WELL-PERCEIVED BY THE COMMUNITY
I	TOUCHES MULTIPLE INDIVIDUALS HAS LONG-TERM IMPACT
II	VISIBLE IMPACT NO OTHER COMPANY FUNDING AREA
I	ASSISTS 18-YEAR-OLDS AND UNDER
IIII	SCIENCE-BASED EDUCATION ITEMS BEYOND NORMAL BUDGET

Tips for Use

- Never use the Multi-Voting technique to pick the winner. Its purpose is to focus discussion on a few critical items.

- The most valuable use of this tool is when multiple votes may be cast for one item. This conveys what is really important to that person.

- It is advisable to have groups mark their votes on a personal sheet of paper prior to marking them on the large sheet of paper or whiteboard as this mitigates a person's tendency to change their vote based on the running tally.

- Further evaluate results of voting by asking, "Would anyone object if we leave off the non-vote getters from the rest of our discussion?" If someone gave all their votes to a particular item, it is extremely important to them and will likely need to be discussed.

Team Handbook, Peter Schultes

Order of Go

Tool Purpose

This tool ensures that there is balanced engagement in your face-to-face or virtual meetings. Rather than leaving the response order to chance (which will favor the more extroverted speaker, the person who is in power or has expertise, or those most fluent in the language being used), the Order of Go establishes who will speak when. As a result, this tool provides an excellent way to ensure inclusion. This technique balances conversation time between dominant and quieter participants and, most importantly, removes the question about who will speak next, a concept known as turn-taking. Used early in the meeting, this tool also increases the likelihood that people will talk more later in the meeting (this is a concept called the activation principle).

This tool can be used throughout a given process but is of particular value in virtual meetings when people are less likely to speak up (even though they have something to say).

Construction Steps

1. Following a question you pose, without taking a breath, identify the order in the following manner: "So I'd like to hear what everyone thinks should be the key focus for this discussion and let's start with Stella on Teams, and then we will do a lap around the table starting with Jose."

2. If someone jumps out of order, ask them to wait, and remind them that you will get to them shortly.

3. If someone declines providing a response, simply acknowledge that you'll check back with them, and move on to the next individual. Then be certain to check back to give them an option to speak later. If they still have nothing to add, that is fine!

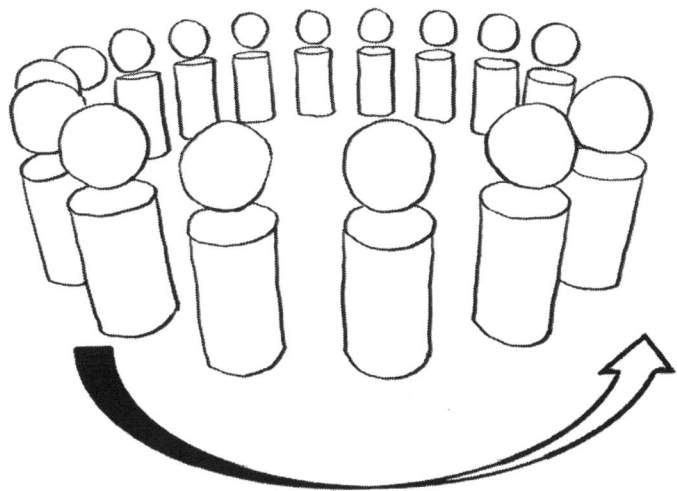

Tips for Use

- In virtual meetings, rather than ask, "Does anyone have any questions?" say, "Let's see what questions are out there. Joe, how about we start with you, and then I'll follow the participant list shown on our screens."
- This is a great tool to equalize talking when you have vocally dominant participants in the room. Without the tool, the more introverted participants or those who are not fluent in the language may simply remain quiet, even though they have something to say.
- Those who are meeting virtually should not always be the last to speak. Start with one person who is dialing in, then return to a person or two in the room, and then seek input from another virtual participant. Remember, your virtual participants are 300% less likely to engage than those in the room.
- If you have a naysayer in the group, structure the Order of Go in such a way that that person will be one of the last to speak. That way they cannot unduly influence the rest of the team and may be influenced themselves!
- If you have a sense that people might want to deliver long-winded speeches, create a limited response frame by stating, "Let's hear your top idea for moving forward." or "Give me just one issue that you'd like to discuss. We'll check back at the end of our lap around the room to see if there is anything that was missed."

Random Word

Tool Purpose

Random Word is a creative thinking tool that stimulates and creates movement in the mind during a creative thinking endeavor. Unlike Brainstorming (which requires the group to think differently based on the responses of others), Random Word uses a literal randomly identifed word to provide the springboard from which a group or individual can generate new alternatives and options.

This tool is closely related to the Innovation Transfer technique (see pages 30–31).

Construction Steps

1. Randomly choose a word from the list provided on the next page (alternatively, open a dictionary to a random page and point to a noun). Chose a different noun if it is too close to the current problem or situation being addressed.

2. Ask the group, "What does this word suggest? What comes to mind? What are some characteristics or features that are associated with this word?" Write the responses to those questions on a large sheet of paper or whiteboard.

3. Circling one of the items listed, ask, "How might this concept apply to our current situation? What features might we employ?"

4. Capture all responses, discuss them, and then use the Multi-Voting Tool (pages 40–41) to narrow down the list.

5. Using an evaluation tool such as the ALU (pages 8–9), assess for use.

	A.	B.	C.
1.	FROST	TOOTHPASTE	TURTLES
2.	BATTERIES	MERCURY	SCISSORS
3.	PLOWS	SAIL BOATS	CANCER
4.	MOLES	POGO STICKS	POPCORN
5.	SNAILS	FROZEN FOOD	PIZZA
6.	WINE	SHUTTERS	CLOCKS
7.	CHAINS	SUBMARINES	SHARK SKIN
8.	VOLCANOS	TELEVISION	X-RAYS
9.	DRILLS	SUPERMAN	LANDFILLS
10.	CAMELS	BEER BOTTLES	EGG SHELLS
11.	CLOUDS	WAFFLE IRONS	CREDIT CARDS
12.	RECIPES	WEDDING RINGS	GRASSHOPPERS
13.	PICTURES	CALENDARS	DENTAL FLOSS
14.	BANKS	COMPOST HEAPS	CLOSETS
15.	SPONGES	DISAPPEARING INK	TANK TREADS

Tips for Use

- There is no such thing as an "unusable" word—discard it only if there is a direct connection with the given situation.
- This is an easy lateral thinking technique.
- Don't let groups directly apply the word to the situation (i.e., if your random word is pizza and your issue is solving juvenile crime, look for solutions beyond feeding pizza to everyone).
- Let people work individually before sharing ideas.
- Since this is a slightly more difficult tool, demonstrate the use of this tool with a non-work issue to first learn how to apply it before tackling a close issue.
- Keep pushing the group to extend themselves, and be sure look for concepts in their responses.

Serious Creativity, Edward de Bono

SCAMPER

Tool Purpose

SCAMPER is an acronym for a list of words that can stimulate new ideas for a given product or process. The letters stand for Substitute, Combine, Adapt, Modify, Put to other uses, Eliminate, and Reverse/Rearrange. These words serve the same creative thinking function as the tools Random Word and Innovation Transfer in that it provides a springboard for thought. The tool is used by asking questions about existing products, processes, or services, using each of the seven prompts noted by the letters in the acronym SCAMPER.

Construction Steps

1. Randomly choose a SCAMPER word on the following page.
2. Apply it to the object or process in question by asking questions such as, "What might we eliminate?" or "How might we substitute?"
3. Capture the responses on a large sheet of paper or whiteboard, or (alternatively) have the group write down their responses on individual sheets, and then collect the responses.
4. Choose another SCAMPER word, and repeat the process.
5. (Optional) Use the Concept Fan tool (pages 12–13) to further expand on your ideas by asking questions such as, "What does the word 'substitute' suggest?" and "What is the broader concept behind eliminating this step? What would that achieve?"
6. Discuss each response, and then narrow down the list of ideas using Multi-Voting (pages 40–41).

SUBSTITUTE
WHAT ELSE INSTEAD?
WHAT OTHER PROCESS COULD BE SUBSTITUTED?

C OMBINE
WHAT CAN BE DONE IN COMBINATION WITH _____?
(CHOOSE SOMETHING)

A DAPT
WHAT ELSE IS THIS LIKE? WHO COULD I EMULATE?
WHERE ELSE COULD THIS BE USED?

M ODIFY, MAGNIFY, MINIFY
WHAT TO ADD? EXAGGERATE? CONDENSE?

P UT TO OTHER USES
NEW WAYS TO USE AS IS? OTHER USES IF MODIFIED?

E LIMINATE
WHAT COULD BE OMITTED? WHAT STEP COULD BE DROPPED?
WHAT FUNCTION COULD BE REMOVED?

R EVERSE, REARRANGE
WHAT OTHER PATTERN? WHAT ROLES COULD BE REVERSED?
WHAT ORDER COULD BE CHANGED?
WHAT IF IT WAS TURNED BACKWARD?

Applied Imagination, Alex Osborn

Spider Diagram

Tool Purpose

The Spider Diagram is a tool that provides a visualization of the attributes of a theme or main idea. It therefore can be used in developing alternative strategies and/or illustrating the differences between strategic themes. This tool is given its name because the key question to be answered lies in the center with the key related themes (4–6) branching out as legs. Along each one of these legs are marks that depict different phases or configurations of the leg theme. When the phases are all connected, it resembles a spiderweb. This provides a simple means of visualizing differences between strategic themes. Because the options (actions) for each focus decision are shown along a continuum, it can also assist with the development of additional options along each leg of the spider diagram.

Construction Steps

1. Label each leg with a focus decision from the decision hierarchy (e.g., market, sales method, structure, pricing).
2. On each leg, create a menu of options (e.g., for the sales method it could be "distributor, own sales force, and partnership"). Be mindful that the top of each leg tends to have a connotation of bigger or greater. Be sure to add options according to that perspective.
3. If only two options have been created for a given leg, ask, "What might lie in the middle of these two options?" to create a third option.
4. Develop a strategic alternative by choosing a set of coherent options from each decision leg, connecting them using a different color for each strategic theme.
5. Challenge the group's thinking by asking questions such as, "What would we achieve if we moved this line to here?" or "Does connecting the lines at the top of every leg suggest a viable strategy?" or "Where are the interdependencies?"

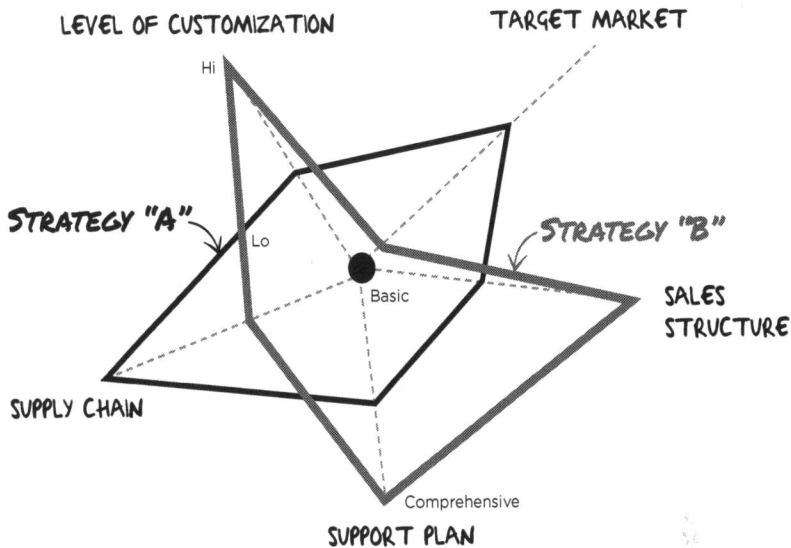

Tips for Use

- People conceptualize differently. Some have a theme in mind and pick the options that fit within the theme, while others start by selecting a set of options that they see fitting together and then label them with a theme. Both methods work. Therefore, facilitate the thinking preferences, not what you think should be done.

- Facilitate dialogue to avoid evaluating strategies prior to the completion of the exercise. Encourage clarifying questions rather than allowing statements of advocacy.

- Use the Values Map outputs as a catalyst. Point to an objective at the bottom of the map and ask, "If this was our most important objective, what strategy would you create to maximize it?"

Strategy Table

Tool Purpose

The Strategy Table is a tool that helps decision-makers create and structure various courses of action. Due to the way it is constructed, it can also be considered an excellent creative thinking tool for developing different strategies, allowing the user to creatively combine the various subdecisions in a coherent fashion.

This tool can also be used to help decision-makers who are stuck in an either-or or first-possible-solution mindset. By asking, "How else might I achieve this desired outcome?" or "What are the subdecisions that are driving the first possible solution mindset?" can help a decision-maker identify heretofore unacknowledged options.

In summary, this powerful creative thinking tool helps a decision-making team explore a breadth of options associated with a potential strategy.

Construction Steps

1. Begin by labeling the decision columns. They represent the different areas of choices associated with your strategic question. For example, a veterinary clinic working on their strategy was exploring decisions related to their growth (stay as-is/aggressive growth), clinic technical capabilities (buy own equipment/partner with area clinic/rely on university), and clinic service offerings (large and small animal/large animal only/equine focus).

2. In each decision column, create a menu of subdecisions/actions.

3. Working across each column, choose an alternative (can be more than one) from each column to create a coherent strategic theme.

4. As an alternative, call out a strategic theme, and then, working across the columns, choose a set of coherent and aligned actions that would achieve that theme.

STRATEGY/THEME	MARKETING CHOICES	R+D OPTIONS	SUPPLY CHAIN OPTIONS	DISTRIBUTION OPTIONS
CIRCLE STRATEGY ○	OPTION 11 △	OPTION 21 □	OPTION 31 ○	OPTION 41 ☆□○
SQUARE STRATEGY □	OPTION 12 ◇○	OPTION 22 ☆○	OPTION 32 ☆△	OPTION 42 ◇△
TRIANGLE STRATEGY △	OPTION 13 ☆	OPTION 23 ◇△	OPTION 33 □	
DIAMOND STRATEGY ◇	OPTION 14 □		OPTION 34	
STAR STRATEGY ☆			OPTION 35	
			OPTION 36 ◇	

Tips for Use

- Similar to the Spider Diagram, people conceptualize differently. Some have a theme in mind and pick the options that fit the theme (working left to right in the table), while others start by selecting a set of options that they see fitting together and then label them with a theme (working right to left). Don't force people to think in just one direction or in your preferred direction. Go with what fits best for the group!

- Facilitate the dialogue to avoid evaluating strategies at this point.

- Use the Values Map (see pages 54–55) as a catalyst. Point to an objective at the bottom of the map, and ask, "If this was our most important objective, what set of actions would you create to maximize it?" Pick an action from each column, and then name the next strategic theme. This is an example of deductive thinking.

- To apply inductive thinking, choose one action from one column. Then ask, "What are actions from each of the other columns that would align with this action?" Once the selections are made, ask, "What might be the rationale for this collection of actions? What does it achieve? What does it not achieve?"

Decision and Risk Analysis, Kenneth Oppenheimer; *DA Tool Kit*, Nick Martino & Katherine Rosback

Three-Column Clarifier

Tool Purpose

The Three-Column Clarifier (3CQ) is a powerful way to transition a meeting from a swirling debate regarding a decision to be made to a more productive way to move forward. The 3CQ helps the group step back from the heat of advocating preferred solutions to explore and consider why the group sees things the way they do and to consider the bigger picture. The value of the tool is that it mirrors how people tend to think rather than forcing them into a process of how they should think. It also helps a group avoid the serious error of too narrowly defining the problem.

Construction Steps

1. Start by asking the group to take a few minutes to share the current situation and the current conversation. Just listen and validate.
2. Use the Order of Go (see pages 42–43) to capture responses to the following questions:
   - "What makes this an issue worth spending time on for you?"
   - "What would the potential impact be if nothing changed?"
   - "What type of outcomes might be different if the issue was solved?"
   - "What ideas are on the table for consideration?"
   - "What issues or risks make it difficult to select the best path forward?"
   - "What unintended consequences (or benefits) could there be?"
3. As the group starts to respond to the questions, create three columns on a whiteboard without labeling them. Capture each answer in 1–2 words in one of the columns based on whether it is:
   - a decision they could make (in left column)
   - a risk or uncertainty they can't control (in center column)
   - an outcome or objective for the future (in right column)
4. After going through the questions, draw attention to where you have captured their comments and label the columns, explaining what a decision, uncertainty/risk, or outcome is, and how it helps categorize the issues in a situation.
5. Ask the group if the summary in the columns captures the situation. Adjust any points of clarification, additions, or deletions.
6. Ask the group, "Given this situation, what do you see is the real question we need to answer? What's the problem we seek to solve?"
7. With this as the Discovery phase, the group will have a solid basis for determining (a) if they need to engage in a simple, moderate, or more complete decision process, and (b) who needs to be involved.

DECISION	RISK YOU CAN'T CONTROL	OUTCOME
SELL THE BUSINESS TO ANOTHER COMPANY	ROLE IN "NEW" COMPANY LEVEL OF INVOLVEMENT BY COMPANY A FINAL NEGOTIATED PRICE	REDUCED STRESS COMPANY SUSTAINABILITY FINANCIAL GAIN
CREATE A PARTNERSHIP	ADDITIONAL LEVEL OF WORK BEST DISTRIBUTION OPTION (SPEED OF PAYMENTS, DISTRIBUTOR RESPONSE) ULTIMATE FINANCIAL SUCCESS OF MERGING	SHARED STRESS COMPANY SUSTAINABILITY FINANCIAL GAIN REDUCED LEVEL OF FULL RESPONSIBILITY
KEEP THE BUSINESS "AS IS"	BEST DISTRIBUTION OPTION ABILITY TO HIRE BETTER PEOPLE	MAINTENANCE OF DECISION-MAKING CONTROL COMPANY SUSTAINABILITY
KEEP BUSINESS, GET A BOARD OF DIRECTORS	BOARD EFFECTIVENESS ULTIMATE VALUE ADDITIONAL LEVEL OF WORK CREATED	REDUCED STRESS COMPANY SUSTAINABILITY FINANCIAL GAIN

Tips for Use

- LISTEN. The value of the tool is that it supports a group's current talk rather than dictating what the talk "should be." If the group has a preference to discuss outcomes, go with it.

- People tend to speak in solutions so start questions such as, "So if it was all up to you right now, what would you do?" or "What ideas are being tossed around right now?" or "What do you wish was different?" Then follow up with the Five Whys tool (see pages 24–25) to further explore their responses.

- Avoid the tendency to be the first to interpret the completed columns with comments such as, "Here is the question that I see you need to answer." Instead, ask the group what *they* see.

©1993 Gary Bush, PhD.

Values Map

Tool Purpose

The Values Map visualizes relationships between the criteria that drive an individual's or group's choice preferences. A critical task in effective negotiation or conflict resolution is to get the whys or ultimate desires of each side into one field of vision. This tool directs the discussion to not just what a person wants but, more importantly, why they want it. What do they hope to achieve? In groups, this tool makes everyone aware of the diversity of objectives and, therefore, why there are fundamental disagreements within the group. By exploring team members' values, preferences, and objectives for a given problem or decision, the Values Map establishes the context for making a decision, visualizes the trade-offs between decisions, and illustrates opportunities for solving the issue in a more holistic way.

Construction Steps

1. Identify the broad challenge or problem statement.
2. Ask, "At the end of the day, what are we hoping to achieve? Why are we doing this?"
3. Ask the group to write down their responses to these questions on sticky notes.
4. Collect sticky notes and ask the team, "Why is this important? What does this achieve?" Place sticky notes underneath the higher level objective to which it leads.
5. Continue to collect sticky notes and ask, "Why is this important?" When you get the answer "Because it just is," you have arrived at what are known as the fundamental objectives. These will be used later as decision criteria to evaluate alternatives.
6. Use arrows to finalize the map of the relationships.

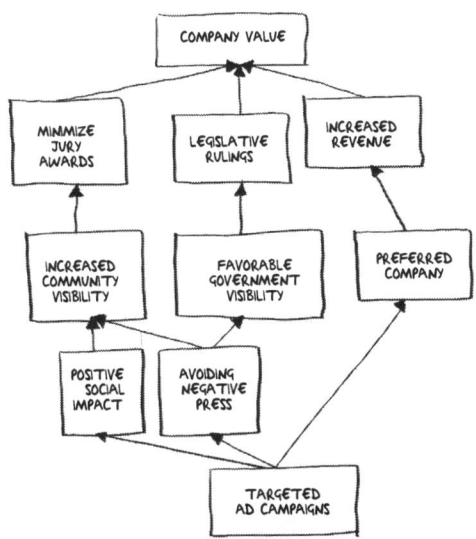

Tips for Use

- Create the map by asking the following questions: "Imagine everything is said and done and you're looking back from the future. What measurable outcomes will tell you if you pursued the best set of ideas today? What are specific outcomes that will indicate success to you? What would be a specific indication of failure?"

- This critical conversation should not be rushed. When exploring a complex decision with 8–10 team members, this discussion could easily take 1–2 hours. The value of the exercise is subsequent understanding of the context for why a decision is important and the alignment of all those involved.

- Separate ends from means objectives by using the Five Whys tool (see pages 24–25). For instance, ask, "Why do we want to have positive social impact?" A response of "Because it increases our community visibility" moves upward to a fundamental objective. Asking, "Why do we want good visibility?" with a response of "Because it can reduce the size of jury awards" moves us even closer to what we are ultimately seeking.

Value-Focused Thinking, Ralph Keeney

WWW.KATHERINEROSBACK.COM

Would building your skills in effectively applying these tools solve the challenges your team currently faces?

To what extent are you frustrated with your team's ability to reach good decisions?

While we have included as much information as possible to help with the application of the tools included, it is impossible to convey in a book the nuances of these tools and how to apply them to your specific situation. Consider one of the following workshops to further develop your skills!

Advanced Facilitation Skills

This highly interactive and engaging two-day workshop has a proven track record of enhancing the skills of anyone working with or on teams. Course highlights include:

- Learning how to design the purposeful meeting.
- Applying methods to mitigate the common decision biases and group dynamics that can hinder good decision-making and inclusion.
- Skill-building in using the tools presented in this book to enhance your facilitation skills.

This widely acclaimed facilitation workshop focuses on application and practice, with each participant having the opportunity to facilitate real-life case studies at various stages of a decision-making or problem-solving process.

Ask the Better Question

- Do you want to improve the uptake of your organizational initiatives?
- Do you seek ways to increase customer or stakeholder engagement?
- Have you struggled with getting buy-in to your new initiative, process, or program?
- Do you find yourself looking to enhance the insights from focus groups?

Rooted in over two decades of extensive research, this workshop is packed with insights and experiences in how to Ask the Better Question. Participants learn the influence that question have on the circuitry of the brain, explore and practice different question structures, and hone skills in using questions to gain better insight, spark innovation, and move people and groups from deeply entrenched positions.

Visit www.katherinerosback.com for more information on additional workshops and service offerings.

Made in the USA
Columbia, SC
29 September 2024